Visual Geography Series®

WALES

...in Pictures

Prepared by
Geography Department

Lerner Publications Company
Minneapolis

Independent Picture Service

Canoeists drag their boats out of the water in Snowdonia National Park in northwestern Wales.

This book is an all-new edition in the Visual Geography Series. Previous editions were published by Sterling Publishing Company, New York City. The text, set in 10/12 Century Textbook, is fully revised and updated, and new photographs, maps, charts, and captions have been added.

LIBRARY OF CONGRESS CATALOGING-IN-PUBLICATION DATA

Wales in pictures / prepared by Geography Department, Lerner Publications Company.
   p. cm. — (Visual geography series)
   Rev. ed. of: Wales in pictures / prepared by Jo McDonald.
   Includes bibliographical references.
   Summary: An introduction, in text and illustrations, to the geography, history, economy, culture, and people of Wales.
   ISBN 0-8225-1877-5
   1. Wales—Juvenile literature. [1. Wales.] I. McDonald, Jo. Wales in pictures. II. Lerner Publications Company. Geography Dept. III. Series: Visual geography series (Minneapolis, Minn.)
DA708.W45 1990
942.9—dc20   90–34972
                             CIP
                             AC

International Standard Book Number: 0-8225-1877-5
Library of Congress Card Catalog Number: 90-34972

VISUAL GEOGRAPHY SERIES®

Publisher
Harry Jonas Lerner
Associate Publisher
Nancy M. Campbell
Senior Editor
Mary M. Rodgers
Editors
Gretchen Bratvold
Dan Filbin
Phyllis Schuster
Photo Researcher
Kerstin Coyle
Editorial/Photo Assistant
Marybeth Campbell
Consultants/Contributors
Barbara Lukermann
Sandra K. Davis
Designer
Jim Simondet
Cartographer
Carol F. Barrett
Indexers
Kristine S. Schubert
Sylvia Timian
Production Manager
Gary J. Hansen

Independent Picture Service

Blackface sheep graze on a hill near Abergavenny, an old city in southern Wales.

Acknowledgments

Title page photo by Christine Pemberton/The Hutchison Library.

Elevation contours adapted from *The Times Atlas of the World*, seventh comprehensive edition (New York: Times Books, 1985).

Courtesy of British Tourist Authority

A sign for Llanfairpwllgwyngyllgogerychwyrndrobwllllantysiliogogogoch – the longest place name on the British Isles – stands above the railway station. Located on the island of Anglesey, the village is often called Llanfair P. G. for convenience.

Contents

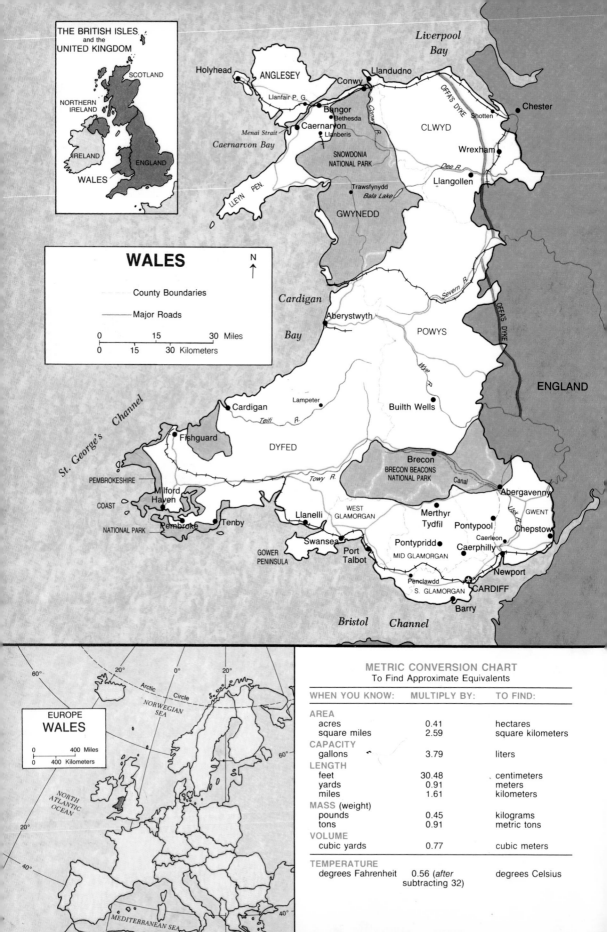

THE BRITISH ISLES
and the
UNITED KINGDOM

SCOTLAND

NORTHERN
IRELAND

IRELAND

ENGLAND

WALES

Liverpool
Bay

Holyhead
ANGLESEY
Llandudno
Conwy
OFFA'S DYKE
Shotten
Chester
Llanfair P. G.
Bangor
Bethesda
CLWYD
Caernarvon
Menai Strait
Llanberis
Wrexham
Caernarvon Bay
SNOWDONIA
NATIONAL PARK
Dee R.
Llangollen
LLEYN PEN.
Trawsfynydd
Bala Lake
GWYNEDD

WALES   N

County Boundaries
Major Roads

0   15   30 Miles
0   15   30 Kilometers

Cardigan
Bay
Aberystwyth
POWYS
Severn R.

ENGLAND

Wye R.
OFFA'S DYKE

Cardigan
Lampeter
Builth Wells
Teifi R.
Fishguard
DYFED
PEMBROKESHIRE
Towy R.
Brecon
BRECON BEACONS
NATIONAL PARK
Canal
Abergavenny
COAST
Milford
Haven
Usk R.
GWENT
Pembroke
Tenby
Llanelli
WEST
GLAMORGAN
Merthyr
Tydfil
Pontypool
Chepstow
NATIONAL PARK
Swansea
Pontypridd
Caerleon
GOWER
PENINSULA
Port
Talbot
MID GLAMORGAN
Caerphilly
St. George's Channel
Penclawdd
Newport
S. GLAMORGAN
CARDIFF
Barry

Bristol Channel

EUROPE
WALES

0   400 Miles
0   400 Kilometers

Arctic
Circle
NORWEGIAN
SEA

NORTH
ATLANTIC
OCEAN

60°
20°
0°
20°
60°
20°
40°
20°
MEDITERRANEAN SEA

METRIC CONVERSION CHART
To Find Approximate Equivalents

WHEN YOU KNOW:	MULTIPLY BY:	TO FIND:
AREA		
acres	0.41	hectares
square miles	2.59	square kilometers
CAPACITY		
gallons	3.79	liters
LENGTH		
feet	30.48	centimeters
yards	0.91	meters
miles	1.61	kilometers
MASS (weight)		
pounds	0.45	kilograms
tons	0.91	metric tons
VOLUME		
cubic yards	0.77	cubic meters
TEMPERATURE		
degrees Fahrenheit	0.56 (after subtracting 32)	degrees Celsius

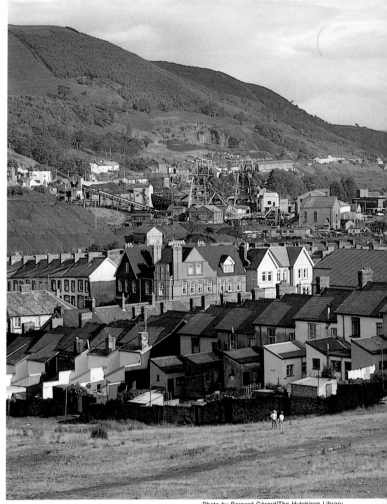

Rows of connected houses snake up and down the hillsides of a town in the Rhondda Valley. In this region of southern Wales, mining was the main occupation throughout the 1800s, and stacks of coal still dominate the landscape.

Introduction

Wales is a small country within the European nation called the United Kingdom of Great Britain and Northern Ireland. England, Scotland, and Wales form Great Britain. Northern Ireland covers the northeastern section of the island of- Ireland. Although united with England since the mid-1500s, Wales also has its own colorful past.

After it was settled by Celtic clans in about 300 B.C., Wales was a target for invaders, including Romans, Normans, and English. Even though the country lost its economic and political independence during these invasions, its people retained a strong cultural identity.

One feature that gives the Welsh a distinctive character is their separate language, which is of Celtic origin. Although English is spoken throughout the country, about 20 percent of the population also use Welsh. Many people in Wales are concerned about the declining number of Welsh-speakers. Efforts to reintroduce the

Signs in Welsh and English welcome visitors who cross the border from England.

Southern Wales became a major coal-exporting center, at one time producing one-third of the world's coal supply.

Investors became very rich from coal mining, while the miners themselves struggled to earn money. Throughout the 1800s and early 1900s—the main period of Welsh mining—laborers took steps to improve their working and living conditions. Their efforts brought voting rights and workers' benefits to the people of Wales.

Since the 1930s, however, mining has declined in Wales. Industries have adapted their machinery to new tasks and have retrained workers for manufacturing jobs. Electronic equipment, car parts, and chemicals are now important manufactured items. An effort has also been made to build factories throughout the country, not just in industrialized southern Wales.

Although high unemployment and the uncertain future of industry in Wales are dominant issues, the country has a history of survival in difficult times. Small and rugged, Wales has maintained its separate identity for more than 2,000 years. Ongoing attempts to preserve the country's traditions and to improve the standard of living are likely to continue in the coming decades.

language in schools and to broadcast in Welsh on television and radio have helped to keep the language alive.

After it united with England in 1536, Wales experienced economic growth and more contact with outsiders than it had in previous centuries. Farming and transportation improved, and investors began to develop the vast deposits of minerals—especially coal—that lay within Wales.

After the mining sector declined in Wales, manufacturing became more important. These steelworks are located in the southeastern part of the country.

6

St. Govan's Chapel is set amid the rocky southwestern coast. To reach the site, visitors must walk down a steep flight of steps. According to local tradition, the small church stands where a holy man named Govan built his humble dwelling in the sixth century.

1) The Land

Wales occupies the western and smallest portion of the island of Great Britain. Located just northwest of mainland Europe, the island has two other parts. Scotland lies in the north, and England is in the south. Great Britain is part of the British Isles, a group of islands that also includes Ireland, the Isle of Man, and many smaller islands.

Wales covers 8,019 square miles of territory, making it roughly the size of the state of Massachusetts. The country includes Anglesey, an island that is separated from Wales by the Menai Strait. West of Anglesey is the island of Ireland, and to the north lies the Isle of Man.

A peninsula, Wales shares its eastern boundary with England. To the north of

Snowdon, the highest point in Wales, juts skyward among 13 other peaks that rise to more than 2,900 feet above sea level. The heights lie in a rugged northwestern region called Snowdonia, where mountain-climbing teams often train before attempting to scale higher summits.

Wales is the Irish Sea, and St. George's Channel and Cardigan Bay stretch to the west. The waters of the Bristol Channel, an arm of the Atlantic Ocean, touch the shores of southern Wales.

Topography

Although mountains and elevated moorland (wet, open wilderness) dominate about two-thirds of Wales, lowlands support the livestock and crop farms that once provided the country's food. The mountains and moors lie in the center, and the lowlands curve along the coast and near several Welsh rivers in the interior.

The main range in Wales is the Cambrian Mountains, which stretch in a wide, north-south block. In northern Wales, the Cambrian peaks form a rugged landscape.

The Cambrian Mountains extend throughout Wales. This section is in the middle of the country, where valleys and fields run between the mountains.

In the center and south, valleys cut between the mountains, offering limited room for farming. The highest point in the range is Aran Mawddwy at 2,970 feet above sea level.

The tallest peak in Wales is Snowdon (3,560 feet), which Welsh-speakers call Eyri, meaning "land of eagles." It lies within Snowdonia, an elevated region west of the Cambrian Mountains. Southeast of these mountains are lower ranges, including the Brecon Beacons and the Black Mountains.

Between the highest mountains are sections of elevated moorland, where wet soil nourishes a variety of rough grasses. Made up of a nearly continuous series of hilltops, the moors are poorly drained. As a result, bogs (areas of damp, spongy terrain) are common. In former times, these bogs provided peat—decomposed plants that, when dried, can be used as fuel.

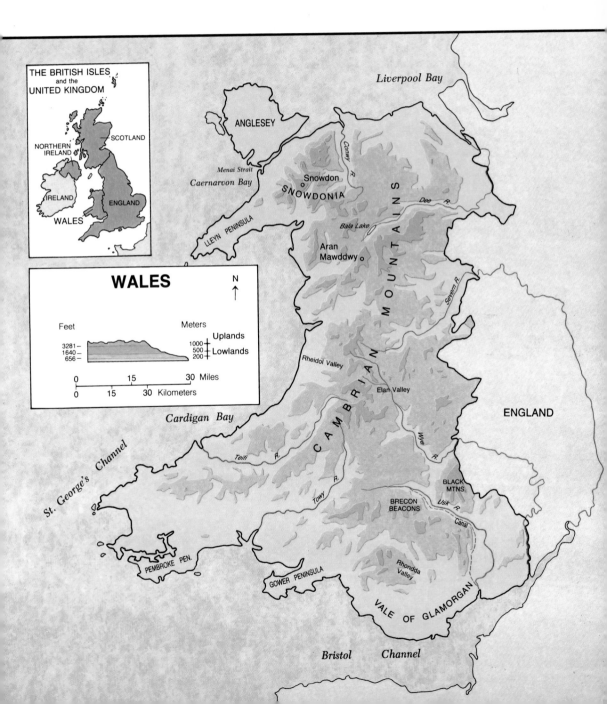

A typical Welsh farmhouse sits at the base of a mountain in northern Wales, with a small waterfall spilling over jagged rocks.

The gently rolling countryside of eastern Wales has long provided some of the best agricultural land in the country. The level terrain has also enabled invaders from England to enter Wales.

Surrounding the broad, mountainous section of Wales are coastal plains and valleys. In some areas, such as the northwest and the south, the coastal plain is wide enough to allow farming. In the west, however, these lowlands are often very narrow. The most fertile farmland lies in the south in the Gower Peninsula and in the Vale (valley) of Glamorgan. Anglesey and inland valleys also offer opportunities for agricultural activities. Other farmable areas exist along the Dee, Severn, Wye, and Usk rivers in the eastern part of the country.

Rivers and Bays

The Dee is the longest river completely within Wales. It starts near Bala Lake—the country's largest inland body of water—and flows through northern Wales into the Irish Sea. During its 70-mile course, the Dee forms part of the boundary between Wales and England. Two longer rivers—the Severn and the Wye—begin in the Cambrian Mountains. A section of each river passes through Wales, but the longest parts are in England. Both rivers empty into the Bristol Channel.

Some waterways have been dammed to produce hydropower. Several shorter streams drain the inland valleys. These rivers include the Conwy in northern Wales, and the Teifi, Towy, and Usk rivers in southern Wales.

Wales has several wide bays, on which large ports, resorts, and fishing centers have developed. Liverpool Bay—which is an arm of the Irish Sea—shapes the northern coast. In the northwest, Caernarvon Bay curves between Anglesey and the Lleyn Peninsula.

Wide Cardigan Bay touches the harbors at Aberystwyth and Cardigan. South of the bay, the land stretches into the broad, irregular Pembroke Peninsula. Milford Haven—one of Britain's main oil ports—juts

The fast-flowing Teifi River rushes through southwestern Wales on its way to St. George's Channel. The river, which is now silted over near its mouth, once contained beavers and salmon.

11

from an inlet along this southwestern peninsula. Along the Bristol Channel in the south are Swansea, Port Talbot, Cardiff—the Welsh capital city—and Newport.

Climate

Wales has a mild, wet climate. The North Atlantic Current—which begins in the warm waters of the Caribbean Sea—heats the water and air surrounding the country. Westerly winds pick up this warm air and blow it inland across Wales. These factors help to moderate temperatures and to carry moisture to every Welsh county.

Altitude also affects temperatures in Wales. The higher elevations—at Snowdon, for example—are colder in both summer and winter than places in the lowlands are. Temperatures at Snowdon usually dip to 30° F in January, the coldest month. In Pembroke on the southwestern coast, the average January temperature is 43° F. In July, the warmest month in Wales, readings at Snowdon reach about 49° F. In Pembroke in the same month, the figures hover around 60° F.

Wales receives large amounts of rainfall throughout the year. The distribution of rain is related to the patterns of the winds that blow across Wales. The heaviest precipitation occurs in upland areas that are in the paths of eastward-moving, rainbearing winds. As the warm winds rise over the mountains, they drop their moisture as rain or snow. Localities on either side of the uplands receive less rain than the mountains do. About 50 inches of precipitation fall annually on the lowland areas. In an average year, the moors get between 50 and 80 inches, and the mountains receive as much as 100 inches.

Courtesy of Britain on View

Windsurfers, sunbathers, and fishermen enjoy the pleasant surroundings of Cardigan Bay. This same area appealed to a very early tourist, Giraldus Cambrensis, who came here in the late twelfth century and later wrote a detailed description of his Welsh travels.

The island of Anglesey—located off the northwestern coast—is also part of Welsh territory. Known as Ynys Môn in the Welsh language, Anglesey has low, heather-covered hills that give way to rolling green fields.

Flora and Fauna

Almost all of Wales's natural vegetation has been destroyed by farming, mining, and human settlement. Three national parks—Pembrokeshire Coast, Brecon Beacons, and Snowdonia—protect the remaining natural areas of Welsh countryside.

Wales contains many species of ferns and mosses, which thrive in the moist soil of the lowlands. The elevated moorlands have short, scrubby vegetation, such as yellow gorse and purple heather. Within the mountainous areas, stands of ash, oak, and pine grow. At the highest elevations, however, only rugged alpine plants can survive. The Forestry Commission has encouraged the planting of new trees, mostly for commercial purposes.

Weasels, badgers, deer, and rabbits live in Wales, as well as in other parts of Great Britain. Some animals, such as foxes, grouse, and partridges, are bred as game for hunting. Nature reserves help to protect some of Wales's birdlife, which includes grebes, herons, mute swans, puffins, gannets, owls, and woodpeckers.

Only a few of Great Britain's animal species are found exclusively in Wales. Among them are red kites—birds of prey that inhabit the wild hillsides and wooded valleys. A superb flier, the red kite feeds on small mammals, birds, and fish. The pine marten, a member of the weasel family, is also a predator and eats mice, squirrels, and rabbits. This mammal sometimes makes its home in tree holes.

Another member of the weasel family found in Wales is the European polecat. Long regarded as harmful to game and poultry, polecats have become extinct in England but still exist in Wales. Living in forested zones, polecats prey on various rodents. The gwyniad—a species of whitefish—swims only in Bala Lake.

13

A pair of wild ponies huddle together in a driving rain in Gwent, Wales's southeasternmost county.

Photo by Sian Roderick

Natural Resources

During the Industrial Revolution of the nineteenth century—when mining and manufacturing expanded—southern Wales prospered. The source of much of its wealth was the coal located in the region's valleys, particularly in the counties of Dyfed, West Glamorgan, Mid Glamorgan, and Gwent. Exploited for decades, supplies of coal are almost exhausted. Only about a dozen mines—out of a maximum of more than 200—still operated in 1990.

In addition to coal, Wales has some limestone and slate, which are used as building materials. These deposits are located in northwestern Wales, particularly near Llanberis. Much smaller quantities of manganese, gold, lead, copper, and zinc also exist in the country. Some of these metals were mined profitably in the 1800s.

Better machinery has improved the working conditions of Welsh coal miners, but they still emerge from the pit covered in coal dust.

Cities

About 75 percent of Wales's 2.8 million people live in or near the industrial cities of southern Wales. Sparsely populated, northern Wales has few large urban centers. Many of Wales's cities rapidly changed from small towns or villages to

Independent Picture Service

14

major manufacturing hubs in the nineteenth century. Since then, the size of Welsh urban areas has decreased as factory closings and unemployment have increased.

Cardiff, the capital of Wales since 1955, lies in the south at the point where three rivers empty into the Bristol Channel. As well as being a governmental center, this city of 270,000 inhabitants is a major seaport, a shipbuilding site, and a university town. In addition to ships, Cardiff's industries produce auto parts, chemicals, electrical equipment, tobacco, beer, and steel. A modern airport at the edge of Cardiff serves travelers within Wales and throughout the United Kingdom. The capital's stadium—known locally as Cardiff Arms Park—is the site of fiercely contested rugby games.

About 45 miles west of Cardiff is Swansea, another important Welsh port and university center. With a population of 183,400, Swansea contains steelworks, oil refineries, and tin-plating plants. Coal mines exist near the city, and Swansea has long been a major coal-exporting harbor. Its modern docks cover an area of more than 250 acres. Air raids during World War II (1939–1945) destroyed central Swansea, which planners have since redesigned to fit the needs of the city's residents.

Situated east of Cardiff, Newport (population 110,000) lies along the estuary of the Severn River, where the river meets the Bristol Channel. The city became prominent during the 1700s and 1800s, when it shipped out steel, iron, and coal that came from mines and factories farther north. Modern Newport has excellent rail links to England and large, up-to-date dock facilities. The city's factories produce steel, aluminum, and chemicals.

Northern Wales is not as industrialized as the south is. The area's main manufacturing town is Wrexham (population 42,000) in northeastern Clwyd county. Wrexham's factories produce beer and

Courtesy of Britain on View

In Swansea, the second largest Welsh city, the Quadrant Centre handles bus services throughout this southern urban area.

Independent Picture Service

The National Library of Wales in Aberystwyth has thousands of Celtic manuscripts, as well as photographs and slides of many aspects of Welsh culture and history.

Cardiff—the Welsh capital since 1955—has rows of terraced houses *(above)* and beautifully designed municipal buildings. The City Hall *(below)*, the National Museum, and the Civic Centre are part of Cathays Park, the focus of official life in the capital.

chemicals, and nearby are facilities that tan leather and mine coal. The coal mines supply fuel for local iron plants and steelworks.

On Cardigan Bay lies Aberystwyth (population 10,000), a seaside resort and university town between northern and southern Wales. Located far from the large urban centers, Aberystwyth has retained its Welsh character. Although small in population, the city contains the National Library of Wales, which houses the largest collection of books and manuscripts in Welsh in the country. The university at Aberystwyth—the oldest in Wales—offers many of its courses in the Welsh language.

This ancient cup, or beaker, is the work of early residents of Wales called the Beaker folk. They lived in the country about 2000 B.C. The cups usually have geometric designs and were buried in ceremonial tombs.

2) History and Government

More than a million years ago, during the last Ice Age, a land bridge connected the British Isles to the European mainland. Archaeological finds—notably at the Paviland Cave in West Glamorgan—suggest that early humans crossed the land bridge into Wales as long as 200,000 years ago. Living in caves for protection from the cold climate, these prehistoric inhabitants used tools and weapons of stone and bone. They hunted now-extinct animals, such as mammoths and woolly rhinoceroses, to feed themselves.

Slowly, the cold climate of Wales changed. Sheets of ice that covered the land began to melt as the Ice Age drew to a close. The melting ice flooded the land bridge, and by 5000 B.C. Great Britain had become an island. As Wales's climate became more mild, its inhabitants moved from caves to outdoor hunting camps. These hunters ventured through dense forests of oak and elm in search of their prey.

Early Inhabitants

Migrations from Europe to Wales occurred again in about 3000 B.C. By 2000 B.C., another group had arrived by sea from what is now West Germany. The newcomers fashioned their tools of bronze and raised crops and livestock on a small scale. These activities, in time, gave the people a more settled way of life.

Scholars have named some of the peoples of this period (called the Bronze Age) the Beaker folk because they buried small jars (or beakers) with their dead. Evidence of the Beaker folk is scattered throughout Wales. Other Bronze-Age groups built large stone monuments and burial chambers along the western coast. Experts speculate that a very organized society was needed to gather the huge stones and to move them to their eventual display sites.

For hundreds of years, the Bronze-Age peoples followed their way of life undisturbed by outside forces. In about 300 B.C., however, another group—known as Celts—came to Wales from northern Europe. A warlike people, the Celts soon conquered the country with superior iron weapons. They grouped themselves into clans, which fought one another for power.

Between 300 B.C. and A.D. 70, these Celtic clans built hill forts and began to raise sheep, cattle, and pigs. Crop farming among the Celts in Wales was limited to land that was well drained. They introduced a strong social organization that included nobles, Druids (scholar-priests), warriors, and common people. By the first century A.D., Celtic art and religion were thriving, and Anglesey had become an important Druidic center.

The Roman Era

During the first century A.D., armies from the Roman Empire, which was centered in what is now Italy, invaded England. Wales escaped the Roman attacks until about A.D. 70. By that time, the Romans had stabilized their control over England (which they called Britannia) and turned their attention to Wales.

Dominated by uplands and inhabited by hardy warriors, Wales was a great challenge for the Roman army. By A.D. 74, the Romans had established two forts. One was at Deva (now called Chester), which lies in the northeast just beyond the modern Welsh border. The other fort stood at Isca Silurum (present-day Caerleon) in the

Photo by E. Emrys Jones/Y Drych

The rugged terrain of Wales helped Celtic warriors to fight the Roman army, which invaded in the first century A.D. Despite strong natural barriers, however, most Welsh Celts eventually came under Roman control.

The ruins of a Roman fort stand in modern Caerleon. Called Isca Silurum in Roman times, the stronghold was the main western base of the Second Legion—a unit of 5,000 experienced soldiers. Their job was to keep an eye on the Silures, the Celtic people who then lived in southern Wales.

south. From these two strongholds, Roman military units kept watch on the restless Celts.

The Romans patrolled Celtic territory for more than three centuries and brought noticeable changes to the region. Well-designed roads connected Deva and Isca Silurum. Improved farming techniques came into use in the Vale of Glamorgan, and better mining methods produced more gold, iron, copper, and lead. Words from Latin, the language of the Romans, found their way into Celtic dialects. In the third century—when the country became part of a separate province called Britannia Prima —Roman missionaries introduced Christianity to the Celts.

Despite its strong cultural and military influence, the Roman Empire began to break up in the fourth century. High-ranking commanders and nobles competed for power, and Rome's control of its far-flung holdings weakened. Roman army units left Britannia Prima to protect other parts of the empire. By the early fifth century, Rome had abandoned its defense of the province.

Celtic Kingdoms

Lacking adequate protection, the Celts in Wales experienced decades of raids and invasions. In the fifth century, Celts from Ireland overran settlements in southwestern Wales. Warring clans from Scotland, called Picts, invaded at about the same time. Angles and Saxons—Germanic peoples from northern Europe—came in the sixth century.

Banding together for defense helped the Celts to foster the first strong kingdoms in Wales. Historians identify Gwynedd and Powys as kingdoms in the north and Dyfed, Gwent, and Morgannwg as southern realms. Smaller domains existed in central Wales. In time, Dyfed would combine with other southwestern realms to form Deheubarth.

These various kingdoms may have arisen initially for defense against the Irish Celts and the Scottish Picts. Later they helped to keep Wales safe from the Anglo-Saxons, who had established several realms in England by the late sixth century. The closest kingdom to the Welsh lands was Mercia, which stretched along the modern boundary with England.

THE CELTIC CHURCH

The arrival of non-Christian Anglo-Saxons ended much of the Celtic culture in England. But in Wales the Celtic way of life—including its language, arts, and Christian traditions—survived. Two reasons for its survival were the Celtic kingdoms that developed and the growth of Celtic Christianity in the sixth century. Monasteries—religious communities of men or women—arose, and small churches dotted the countryside. Missionaries preached throughout Wales, and some of these holy people were regarded as saints. A Celt named David became the patron saint of Wales.

Meanwhile, in England, the Anglo-Saxons had accepted the Roman style of Christianity. The rules and channels of authority of this branch of the faith were different from the Celtic variety. The Roman Catholic Church wanted the Celts to recognize Roman rules and leaders. The Celts of Wales formally agreed to this change in the eighth century. The new arrangement made Wales officially more

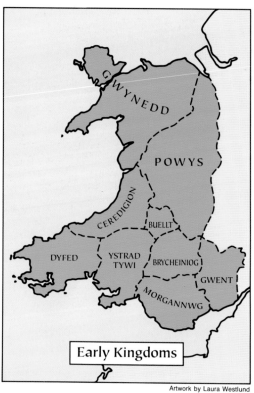

Artwork by Laura Westlund

Beginning in the sixth century, separate Welsh kingdoms took shape, but internal and external warfare made them unstable.

Courtesy of Britain on View

A Christian Celt named David established a church in southwestern Wales in the sixth century. After his death, he became the country's patron saint, and a large cathedral replaced the earlier structure. St. David's Cathedral developed as both a center of Christianity and a place of pilgrimage in Wales.

20

Courtesy of Britain on View

Offa's Dyke—an earthen barrier—runs in a north-south direction in eastern Wales. Built in the eighth century by an Anglo-Saxon king, the dyke marked the border between his kingdom and the Celtic realms in Wales.

similar to Europe, but Celtic traditions remained popular in many areas of the country.

The connection with Europe did not make the Celtic kingdoms part of the Anglo-Saxon domains in England. In fact, King Offa, the leader of Mercia in the eighth century, built an earthen wall—Offa's Dyke—to mark the boundary between his kingdom and the Celtic lands. The Anglo-Saxons did bring about one long-term change in Celtic life. In Anglo-Saxon, from which the English language developed, the people west of Offa's Dyke became *Wealh*, or "foreigners." Since then, they have been referred to as Welsh.

Search for Unity

Although separate kingdoms existed throughout Wales, they were not stable. They warred against one another as much as they did against outside forces. In addition, the royal dynasties (families of rulers) that controlled the realms began to die out, which further weakened Wales. Three strong leaders emerged from the disorder, and each attempted to unite the entire country under his rule.

Through marriages and battles, Rhodri Mawr (Rhodri the Great), king of Gwynedd, gained power in central and northern Wales. By the middle of the ninth century, only southern realms remained beyond his authority. The king successfully fought the Vikings—raiders from Denmark—who made sweeping attacks on coastal settlements on Anglesey. Killed in battle against the Anglo-Saxons in 878, Rhodri is remembered by Welsh people as one of the first leaders to try to unite Wales.

Territories ruled by Rhodri Mawr

TWIXT WYE & SEVERN

BUELLT

DYFED

BRYCHEINIOG

GWENT

MORGANNWG

Wales in the time of Rhodri Mawr

Artwork by Laura Westlund

The first Welsh ruler to have control over a large part of Wales was Rhodri Mawr, who ruled in the ninth century.

After Rhodri's death, Wales was again divided into many small kingdoms until the tenth century. At that time, Rhodri's grandson, Hywel Dda (Hywel the Good), king of Gwynedd, gained control of most of the country. By marriage Hywel acquired Deheubarth, and by 950 he ruled Powys in the north as well. To govern his enlarged realm, Hywel Dda organized the laws of Wales into a single legal code. It described how property was to be inherited. The code also recognized all children—whether born within or outside of marriage—as a father's legal heirs.

After Hywel died, his successors separately ruled parts of his larger kingdom. In the eleventh century, Gruffydd ap Llywelyn seized Gwynedd, Powys, and Deheubarth from Hywel's descendants. A ruthless ruler, Gruffydd united all of Wales for the first time. He killed potential rivals, and his own soldiers eventually betrayed him to his enemies in 1063.

When Rhodri, Hywel, and Gruffydd governed Wales, the country was made up of remote rural settlements. Farmers planted crops where the soil was fertile, but most farms raised livestock. Although small in size, the main Welsh kingdoms had a strong cultural life. Bards, or singer-poets, recorded the history of the realms in song and verse. The kings spent large sums of money to support monasteries, which acted as centers of education.

In other parts of Wales, less powerful kingdoms rose and fell in the tenth and eleventh centuries. War broke out continually between kings and nobles and between brothers or cousins seeking power. In search of military protection, some of these kingdoms allied with the Anglo-Saxons, who were now molded into a single, strong realm called England.

English armies raided eastern Wales at will and often controlled land west of Offa's Dyke. In time, Welsh rulers decided that they could preserve their independence only by recognizing England's authority. By the mid-eleventh century, Welsh kings regularly appeared at the English court to swear oaths of loyalty—an action that was meant to keep the English out of Wales.

The Norman Conquest

In 1066 armies from Normandy (now part of France) conquered England. Under William the Conqueror, who became the first Norman king of England, Norman laws, language, and government replaced the English system. Like the English,

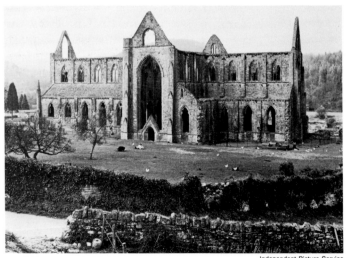

Independent Picture Service

Norman nobles took over parts of southern and eastern Wales in the eleventh century. Called Marcher lords, these nobles built castles as well as monasteries. Walter de Clare, Marcher lord of Chepstow in the southeast, founded Tintern Abbey in 1131. Now an attractive ruin, the abbey once housed dozens of Cistercian monks.

By the early 1200s, Llywelyn the Great of Gwynedd controlled two-thirds of Wales. Surrounding his lands on two sides were Marcher lords. Llywelyn used his skill as a commander and diplomat to achieve unity within Wales. By marrying most of his children to English and Norman nobles, he balanced Welsh independence against Norman demands for submission.

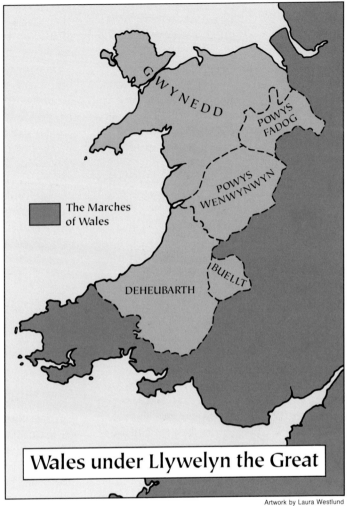

The Marches of Wales

Wales under Llywelyn the Great

Artwork by Laura Westlund

the Normans regarded Wales as part of their domain. But unlike the conquest of England—which was decided in one battle in 1066—the takeover of Wales was accomplished gradually.

King William allowed his strongest nobles to claim land along the Welsh border. In this area, known as the Marches (from the French word for "frontier region"), Norman armies seized Welsh lands. Welsh leaders fought back, using their skilled foot soldiers and knowledge of the rugged terrain to deliver strong attacks. In time, however, the Marcher lords (as the nobles came to be called) gained authority over eastern and southern Wales.

For 200 years after the Norman Conquest, Welsh kings avoided further invasions through marriages, alliances, battles, and oaths of loyalty. These efforts allowed the Welsh to maintain their own laws, language, and arts amid Norman culture. During the twelfth and thirteenth centuries, the kingdom of Gwynedd—protected by the mountains of northwestern Wales—became a stronghold of Welsh self-rule.

THE TWO LLYWELYNS

Among the most outstanding of Gwynedd's kings was Llywelyn the Great. He used war, political marriages, and diplomacy to bring Wales under his leadership

Llywelyn's grandson and namesake was the last Welsh Prince of Wales. A stone marks the spot near Builth Wells where Llywelyn II was killed in 1282. Before his death, he succeeded in expanding his grandfather's possessions, an achievement that put him in serious conflict with the English king Edward I.

NEAR THIS SPOT
WAS KILLED
OUR PRINCE
LLYWELYN
1282

Courtesy of Britain on View

in the early thirteenth century. By 1230 all other Welsh kings recognized Llywelyn as their overlord (supreme ruler).

The nearly 40-year reign of Llywelyn was followed by a short period of family warfare, when his sons competed for power. By 1255 his grandson, also named Llywelyn, had retaken Gwynedd and began to enlarge the realm eastward and southward. By 1262 Llywelyn II had freed the other Welsh kingdoms from Norman control, and in 1267 he was acknowledged as Prince of Wales by the Norman king of England, Henry III.

Helping Llywelyn in these endeavors was the fact that England was experiencing its own problems. Nobles under Henry III were challenging the way that he ran the country. The king could not deal both with civil war and with Wales. In addition, Henry did not have enough money to pay for a war in Wales. As a result, Llywelyn II was able to achieve internal unity as well as to get England's recognition of his authority.

Llywelyn's success, however, spurred England to take action. In 1272, when Henry III's son Edward I inherited the English throne, Llywelyn refused to make the usual oath of loyalty. Edward's armies invaded Wales, and Llywelyn's troops lost battles against better-equipped English soldiers. Under the terms of the Treaty of Aberconwy in 1277, the English drastically reduced the size of Llywelyn's kingdom.

Remaking Wales

Llywelyn II retained the title Prince of Wales and again tried to make war against Edward in 1282. In response, the king sent another army to crush Gwynedd. The Welsh leader was killed in a skirmish, and the fate of Wales was in Edward's hands.

The king seized all the land in Wales. He reserved some territory for the Marcher lords and built strong castles to defend his new acquisition. He chose not to unite Wales with England, but rather to add the country to his list of outlying lands. To prevent rebellions, Edward stripped the descendants of Llywelyn the Great and Llywelyn II of their inheritance. The king eventually gave the title Prince of Wales to his eldest son. Thereafter, Wales was a principality (realm of a prince) that belonged to male heirs of the English throne.

Edward I brought Wales under the authority of the Statute of Rhuddlan in 1284. This law divided royal territory—separate from the Marcher lands—into shires (counties) according to the English style of administration. Some ancient Welsh customs, such as those regarding landownership, remained in force, but

Edward I defeated the Welsh in the 1280s. The construction of a string of castles, many of which still stand, followed his victories. Caernarvon Castle was begun in 1283 to enforce the English king's power. The structure, which cost roughly $3 million to build, was completed in about a decade. Edward's eldest son, who would later assume the title Prince of Wales, was born here in 1284.

Courtesy of Britain on View

Courtesy of British Tourist Authority

Harlech Castle, also founded in 1283, is another Edwardian defensive site. Perched on a mass of rock, the castle remained full of troops for several centuries after Edward's death in 1307.

25

English common law came into use in the courts of Wales.

Although isolated rebellions against English rule occurred in the 1300s, for the most part the Welsh reluctantly accepted the new situation. The wealthy, landowning descendants of the former kings of Wales became the nobility of the principality. But few Welsh nobles gained positions of power in the new order, and the people were not treated as equals. As a result, discontent increased, and the idea of rebellion remained popular.

THE GLENDOWER REBELLION

In the late 1300s, a Welshman named Owen Glendower gave voice and action to Welsh grievances against the English. Descended from the royal houses of Powys, Deheubarth, and Gwynedd, he also had learned English ways while a court official in London, the English capital city.

Independent Picture Service

Owen Glendower, a Welsh landowner, led a popular rebellion against the English in the early 1400s. He had the support of dissatisfied English nobles, as well as of ordinary Welsh people. Although Glendower's revolt eventually failed, he took Harlech Castle, which became the headquarters of his short-lived administration.

Upon returning to Wales to oversee a small piece of land, Glendower disputed his boundary with his neighbor, a Marcher lord. This disagreement sparked a rebellion that raged throughout Wales in the early 1400s. After defeating the Marcher lord, Glendower began to bring Wales under his control. The landowning Welsh families made Glendower Prince of Wales. He then called a parliament into session, created a civil service, and marked the borders of Wales.

Although civil war had broken out in England, English leaders could not allow Glendower to establish Wales as an independent country. The English king, Henry IV, assembled an army that subdued Wales. By 1410 Glendower had fled, and the king had seized rebel lands. He enacted laws that greatly reduced the wealth, status, and liberty of Welsh people. They could not own military weapons, gather in public places, or hold office. The Welsh could not testify at the trial of an English person nor own land. In some districts, even citizenship was withdrawn.

CIVIL WAR AND HENRY TUDOR

For a time, Glendower's rebellion distracted the English from their own civil war. The struggle resumed in England between the Yorkists and the Lancastrians, who were actually two branches of the same ruling family. The person who finally ended the war was a Welshman named Henry Tudor.

Henry, a Lancastrian, had ties to both the Welsh and English royal families. He landed with his troops in 1485 at Milford Haven in southwestern Wales. Flying a flag that carried a red dragon (a traditional Welsh symbol), Henry joined his army to forces gathered in Wales. Together the Welsh and Lancastrian soldiers defeated the Yorkists at the Battle of Bosworth in England in 1485.

Because of Henry's victory, the English Parliament proclaimed him king of England. He came to the throne as Henry VII

Independent Picture Service

Born in Pembroke Castle in southwestern Wales, Henry Tudor had a claim to the English crown through his mother and ties to the Welsh royal family through his father. In 1485, after winning a battle against English forces, he gained the English throne as Henry VII.

and married the niece of the last Yorkist ruler, combining the Houses of Lancaster and York in a Tudor alliance.

The Tudor Dynasty

Although in control of England, Henry Tudor did not forget his homeland. Many Welsh people went to London and gained positions of power in the government. The king annually celebrated St. David's Day on March 1, when members of his court wore a traditional Welsh symbol—the leek (a type of onion)—in their caps.

The greatest changes for Wales, however, came during the reign of Henry VII's son, Henry VIII. This monarch combined Wales and England through the Acts of Union of 1536 and 1543. These laws removed some of the worst limitations imposed after the Glendower rebellion and took away the power that the Marcher lords had over lands in the east and south. Wales was reorganized into 13 shires, which generally followed the boundaries of the country's ancient realms. These 13 counties were allowed to send representatives to the English Parliament.

The Acts of Union had long-range effects on Welsh identity. Although the people of England and Wales were now legally equal, the Welsh language could not be used in official circles or in the courts. The tenth-century legal code of Hywel Dda was replaced with English laws. The Welsh nobility and landowners drew closer to England, and a gap emerged between these groups and ordinary Welsh society. For the wealthy, life was now focused on London, and Welsh culture was neglected.

Another change that occurred in Wales originated in Henry VIII's private life and had little to do with the Acts of Union. It was traditional in both Wales and England for a male to inherit a kingdom, but Henry VIII and his wife had no sons. Henry asked the Roman Catholic pope to dissolve his marriage so that he could marry someone else. The pope refused. In response Henry declared himself head of the church in England in 1534 and divorced his wife.

Henry VIII's successors formalized this religious break by creating the Church of England (or Anglican Church) as a separate organization. England and Wales no longer had ties or obligations to the Roman Catholic Church. Under the orders of the new church, Welsh scholars translated the Bible and the Book of Common Prayer into Welsh. For the first time, Welsh churchgoers could hear services in their native tongue.

The 1600s

Because of their Welsh ancestry, the monarchs of the Tudor dynasty enjoyed the loyalty of Welsh people at all levels of society. In the 1600s, when the Stuarts of

Civil war broke out in England in the 1640s and spread to Wales. The Welsh were generally supportive of the Royalists, who fought for the monarchy. The forces of Parliament under Oliver Cromwell *(left)* eventually overcame the Royalists, many of whom fled to Europe. By 1660, however, King Charles II *(right)* had reclaimed his family's throne.

Scotland inherited the English throne, the Welsh supported the new rulers. In part, Welsh reaction stemmed from the fact that the first Stuart king of England, James I, was the great-great-grandson of Henry Tudor.

The loyalty of the Welsh persisted through the quarrels over money and authority that James and his successor, Charles I, had with Parliament. When the disagreements developed into civil war in the 1640s, most of the Welsh supported the king. Battles occurred along the eastern border. By late 1644, eastern Wales was in the hands of Parliament's supporters.

In the south—a strategic area because of its access to the sea—successes by parliamentary forces encouraged the southern shires to side with Parliament in 1645. Northwestern Wales held out the longest, but by 1647 this area and the king were in the hands of the Parliamentarians. In 1649 they beheaded Charles I after a public trial.

For more than a decade, Wales was part of a republic, not a monarchy. Heading this new form of government was Oliver Cromwell, a skilled military commander who followed a strict Protestant religious sect called Puritanism. To instill Puritan ideas in the Welsh population, Cromwell's Parliament ordered schools to be built and teachers to be trained. Education was free, and girls as well as boys were encouraged to attend classes.

Cromwell's Puritan beliefs also caused some unpopular changes, such as censorship and illegal imprisonment. These actions doomed his efforts to establish a permanent republic. Cromwell died in 1658, and by 1660 Parliament had restored the monarchy under Charles I's son, Charles II. As strong backers of the earlier royalist cause, the Welsh generally supported the new king.

During the brief Cromwellian period, an educational system was established in Wales. In addition, although Puritanism itself had not become very popular, the idea of supporting Protestant religions other than the established Church of England took root. Through these two pathways—education and religion—Wales entered a new phase of its development in the 1700s. At the same time, England, Wales, and Scotland were formally combined to form the United Kingdom of Great Britain (also called Britain).

Social and Economic Changes

By the 1700s, Welsh society consisted of two layers—a wealthy, English-speaking upper section and a poorer, Welsh-speaking lower layer. Members of the English-speaking upper class had strong ties to the Anglican Church and to the best English schools. Their incomes generally came from farming their land and from rents paid by tenant farmers. People in the lower class—mostly farmers and farm laborers—had only recently been offered schooling. Their instructors usually were enthusiastic preachers who taught the Welsh people in their own language.

The upper class held all political power, sending delegates to Parliament in London. The mass of Welsh people could not vote. When political parties began to form in Britain, most of the legislative members from Wales were Tories. They supported the monarchy, the landowners, and the Church of England. The opposition party —the Whigs—favored the expansion of parliamentary power at the expense of the monarch and the church.

Far from the politics and entertainments in London, Wales lacked some attraction

In the 1700s, the lives of high-born members of Welsh society were very similar to the lifestyles of rich English people. Both Welsh and English aristocrats owned large country homes, where mounted hunters and their dogs gathered to chase foxes for a day of sport.

The Methodists—a Protestant sect—had considerable influence over Welsh people in the 1700s and 1800s. The faithful built plain Methodist chapels throughout the country, where teaching as well as preaching were done in the Welsh language.

available in England. Wales's isolation helped Methodists, Baptists, and other religious groups that did not conform (agree) with established Anglican policies to change Wales. Called nonconformists, these groups built hundreds of chapels, which eventually replaced Anglican churches as meeting places. Ordinary Welsh people made up the congregations and used the Welsh language in their services. Nonconformist preachers became the primary entertainers, teachers, political activists, and advisers in Wales.

THE INDUSTRIAL REVOLUTION

Alongside the rise of a chapel-dominated Welsh society came the development of mining industries. The large deposits of coal, copper, iron, slate, and lead in Wales were well known. In the eighteenth century, inventors came up with better tech-

niques for extracting these materials, and industrialists found new ways to use the resources. Both of these factors expanded mining, changing Wales from a minor farming region to a major industrial area by the nineteenth century. These events were part of a transformation—known as the Industrial Revolution—that was taking place throughout Britain.

At the beginning of the nineteenth century, coal extraction became more important than all other types of mining in Wales. At first, miners hauled away the coal that lay closest to the surface. The coal was burned to power steam-driven machines, including pumps that cleared water from shafts so that deeper mines could be drilled. Coal fueled huge furnaces for manufacturing and ran equipment that crushed iron ore before it was smelted (a process that melts metals). Investors built ironworks near the coal deposits in southern Wales, principally in the booming town of Merthyr Tydfil, which had once been a small village.

People from rural Wales moved to the south, where rows of houses were built for the workers and their families. New technologies enabled mining shafts to descend ever deeper into the earth. The safety lamp, which reduced the possibility of fire, allowed miners to work at lower depths. Improved refining methods created markets even for poor-quality coal, and the industry expanded further.

Increases in coal production and exports went hand in hand with improvements in transportation. Welsh roads were paved, and canals connected Pontypool with Newport and Merthyr Tydfil with Cardiff.

Tramways—sets of iron rails on which horses pulled vehicles—also aided travel. In time, railways replaced the tramways. Many of the new tracks were made in Wales.

Reforms and Riots

Coal brought great wealth to investors, mine owners, and landlords. For workers, the story was different. Wages were low, and working conditions were dangerous. Men, women, and children were exposed to polluting gases and dust that caused lung diseases and other health problems. Limited space in the mines often forced laborers to work for hours in uncomfortable, cramped positions. Mining accidents caused fatal and crippling injuries.

Courtesy of British Coal Corporation

The Welsh mining industry became very active in the 1800s. Mines in the Rhondda Valley in southern Wales employed large numbers of people who risked injury and even death to dig out the coal. Roughly cut logs shored up the walls of underground pits. Sometimes the walls collapsed, burying the workers alive.

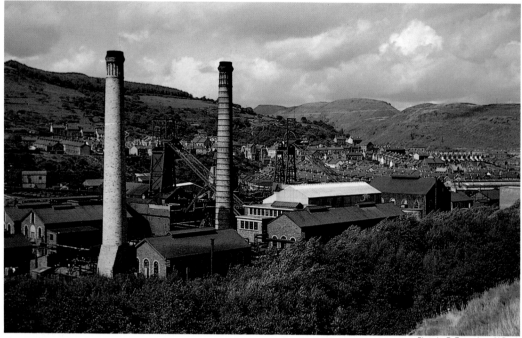

Photo by E. Emrys Jones/Y Drych

For centuries, Merthyr Tydfil had been a small town. When the industrial boom began to hit Wales, the town grew and prospered because of its deposits of iron ore. Ironworks and steelworks sprang up, and these factories produced large amounts of machinery and goods. By the mid-1800s, Merthyr Tydfil was the largest city in Wales.

In the 1830s, some of these problems and dangers came to the attention of Parliament. New labor laws brought the workers some protection. More men were allowed to vote, giving a larger section of the population a voice to encourage change. For some of the Welsh workers, however, these reforms were not enough, and they expressed their dissatisfaction with existing conditions. Among these groups were the Chartists and the Rebecca rioters.

The Chartists, who were generally laborers, took their name from the People's Charter that they published in 1838. It listed the human freedoms to which they

In the 1840s, farmers rioted against taxes and tolls they had to pay. The leaders of the movement took their inspiration from a biblical activist named Rebecca. Some of the male Rebecca rioters even dressed in women's clothing when they destroyed local tollgates.

Photo by Bettmann/Hulton

32

In 1910 David Lloyd George, legislative member for Caernarvon, walked with his wife to Parliament. After they arrived, he delivered his national budget as head of the Exchequer (national treasury).

felt they were entitled, including voting rights for all men and the option for non-landholders to seek seats in Parliament.

Named after a biblical heroine, the Rebecca rioters were mostly farmers from southwestern Wales who experienced hard times in the early 1840s. Supporters of the movement rioted to protest various fees they had to pay for services in their communities. For example, farmers were charged money to pass through tollgates when they moved their goods or livestock to market. The farmers also had to pay a tax to the Anglican Church, even though they belonged to nonconformist chapels.

Alongside the Welsh workers, English laborers pressed for reforms, resulting in a public health act and further parliamentary changes in the 1860s and 1880s. Political shifts accompanied these social reforms. The Tories emerged as the Conservative party, and the Whigs became the Liberal party. These two groups followed one another in power and passed legislation to attract new voters. The governments sponsored laws that gave voting rights to workers and that set up a national educational system.

Between 1880 and 1922, Wales established itself as a Liberal stronghold, sending many Liberal members of Parliament to London. One of the party's most gifted speakers was David Lloyd George—a young Welsh lawyer from a working-class background.

In time, a third political organization—the Labour party—formed from workers' unions. It represented the interests of the working class. Some of the party's goals, such as nationalization (transferring private property to state ownership), were far different from the ideas of the Liberals and the Conservatives.

The new party found Welsh supporters among discontented laborers in Cardiff, Merthyr Tydfil, Swansea, and Newport. In the late 1800s, these cities became separate administrative units that could send their own representatives to Parliament. In 1900 Merthyr Tydfil elected Keir Hardie as the first Labour member of Parliament in Britain's history.

Competition and Conflict

At about the same time, the output of Welsh coal mines reached roughly 40 million tons per year—enough to supply one-third of the world's needs. Slate quarries, tin-plating factories, and other industrial activities further contributed to the economic strength of Wales. During this period, Britain made alliances to maintain its control of world markets and European power. Britain had the strongest navy in the world, and its economic activities touched six continents. Competing with Britain was Germany, which had rapidly industrialized and improved its military strength in the late 1800s.

Workers' needs and trade developments challenged the Liberal government that came to power in 1905. David Lloyd George entered the national cabinet as head of the Board of Trade, and by 1908 he was in charge of the treasury department. Lloyd George's first budget—called the People's Budget—included old-age pensions and payments for sick and unemployed laborers. Although the budget met a lot of resistance, Parliament eventually passed it, and workers finally had some protection against hard times.

A memorial to a young Welshman named Hedd Wyn stands in Trawsfynydd, northern Wales. In 1917, during World War I, this young writer entered his works in the National Eisteddfod. At this festival of Welsh culture, he hoped to win honors as the finest bard (singer-poet). While serving in Belgium, Wyn was killed without knowing he had won the prize for poetry.

By 1914—when Welsh mines produced an all-time high of 57 million tons of coal—Germany was Britain's main rival for economic and political influence. In that year, Germany's ally Austria attacked Serbia in eastern Europe. Because of the United Kingdom's military agreements, this action brought Britain and its allies into World War I. Thousands of Welshmen—from every class and profession—enlisted or were drafted to fight in the global conflict. Some Welshwomen took over factory jobs to produce war supplies.

Lloyd George was a major force in the British cabinets that made decisions during World War I. He became minister of munitions (war supplies) in 1915 and secretary of war in 1916. Later that year, Lloyd George accepted the post of prime minister—the nation's chief decision maker. Although the war initially had much popular support, the length of the conflict weakened public backing. By 1918, when Germany was finally defeated, Britain had lost more than 800,000 people.

The Postwar Period

The war put enormous pressure on the mineral resources of Wales, whose coal mines had been worked unceasingly for more than a century. Supplies of coal were beginning to decline. In addition, ships were changing from coal-fired to oil-burning engines. These factors reduced the demand for Welsh coal.

After the war, returning Welsh soldiers expected to share in the prosperity of peacetime. Their expectations were not met, however, as the industrial sector declined. In the 1920s, workers participated in regional strikes and hunger marches and increased their support for the Labour party. It replaced the Liberal party as the main political organization in Wales.

An even greater economic downturn—the global depression of the 1930s—hit Wales hard. Unemployment rose sharply, and Welsh people experienced widespread

Residents of Cardiff viewed the damage done to their street after German bombers had blitzed the city during World War II (1939–1945).

suffering as thousands of families lacked money for food and shelter. Many people left the country to seek opportunities abroad or in England. Amid the economic depression, however, a new political and cultural force emerged—Plaid Cymru (the Welsh Nationalist party). Its aims included self-rule for Wales, the preservation of the Welsh language, and pacifism (opposition to war).

WORLD WAR II AND ITS AFTERMATH

The members of Plaid Cymru, as well as other Welsh people, watched as events in Europe led to the outbreak of World War II in 1939. In that year, Nazi Germany attacked Poland, and the British government declared war against Germany. Again Welshmen and Welshwomen enlisted or worked in factories.

In their attacks on the British Isles, the Germans did not spare southern Wales and its industrialized areas that produced weapons and war machinery. Defensive stations were in place on Anglesey and the Gower Peninsula, and Cardiff had its own radar station to detect enemy aircraft. Despite these measures, Cardiff and Swansea were heavily bombed between 1940 and 1943. In that year, the tide of the European war began to turn in favor of Britain and its allies. By 1945 the war had ended, and Germany was defeated.

Many feared that the widespread unemployment of the 1930s would return in the postwar period. The Labour party won the national elections in 1945. To strengthen the economy, the new government enacted programs that broadened the industrial base of southern and northern Wales. By the 1950s, successful businesses in Swansea, Cardiff, and Newport were making vehicle parts, electrical equipment, and chemicals. The earnings of Welsh people

35

rose, and they could now afford to own their homes and to buy cars.

Another of the government's programs brought many privately owned industries, such as coal and steel, under the authority of the state. This move further tied the Welsh economy to England's. The Labour government also enacted broad social legislation that improved living conditions for workers in the United Kingdom. One of the chief architects of these plans was a former Welsh coal miner named Aneurin Bevan. As minister of health, Bevan designed the National Health Service, which offered most medical services at minimal cost to patients.

This young welder works at a car factory in Llanelli. In the 1960s and 1970s, the British government encouraged manufacturers to locate new plants in Wales.

Recent Events

For some Welsh people, the new legislation threatened the very things that gave Wales an identity and culture separate from those of England or Scotland. A telling statistic was the drop in the number of people who spoke Welsh. In the early 1900s, Welsh was the first language of more than half of all Welsh people. In the 1960s, only about 25 percent of the population could speak Welsh.

Plaid Cymru stepped up its efforts to preserve Welsh culture and won its first seat in Parliament in 1966. Another organization, the Welsh Language Society, pledged to take direct action to help Welsh to survive in Wales. Welsh-speaking youths were the main members of the society. Their secret patrols painted over English place names on signposts and destroyed equipment that brought English broadcasts into Wales.

In 1967 Parliament passed the Welsh Language Act, which made Welsh equal to English in all legal situations. For the first time in more than 400 years, Welsh could be used in court. A later agreement provided for a Welsh television channel. Other legislation replaced the old shires established by Edward I with eight counties whose names evoked the ancient Welsh kingdoms. This change was not well re-

Since 1301 British monarchs have given the title Prince of Wales to their eldest sons. Here, Queen Elizabeth II places a crown on the head of her son Charles during ceremonies in 1969 that formally invested him with this title. The event took place in Caernarvon Castle, where the first English Prince of Wales was born. Because of growing Welsh nationalism, there was much public feeling for and against the investiture.

ceived in Wales, however, since it erased nearly 700 years of loyalty to the Edwardian shires. In 1969 Edward's remote descendant Prince Charles—eldest son of Britain's Queen Elizabeth II—was formally invested with the symbolic title Prince of Wales.

In the 1970s, Plaid Cymru continued to win seats in irregularly scheduled elections to replace members of Parliament. This development alarmed the Labour party, which had long been able to count on the support of Welsh voters. In a bid to regain Welsh backing, the Labour government, which was plagued with strikes and rising unemployment, organized a public vote offering Wales its own legislative assembly. The government chose March 1, 1979—St. David's Day—for the vote. A majority voted against the option that would have

given Wales limited self-rule. Debates still take place about the reasons for the rejection, but economic considerations probably played a large part in the decision.

Throughout the 1980s, economic concerns—including rising unemployment— and the nationalist issue have both been important. The future of Wales depends partially on finding ways to give Welsh industry more flexibility and diversity. This could be done by attracting a greater number of businesses or by broadening the types of goods being produced in Wales. These actions may help to lower the unemployment rate, which stood at more than 10 percent throughout the 1980s. Accompanying these efforts, however, is the desire to preserve the elements that make Wales a separate country—its language and traditions.

In 1972 at the University of Wales in Bangor protesters demonstrated against the arrival of a British official to give a lecture in English. Members of the crowd carry signs that say "Do everything in Welsh" and that express other anti-English views.

Government

The United Kingdom has no written constitution. Instead, various parliamentary acts and common laws form the basis of government. Although symbolically headed by a monarch, the nation is governed by Parliament and by a cabinet made up of members of Parliament (MPs). The monarch's eldest son is given the title Prince of Wales, but he does not own or run the country. The prime minister is the most powerful figure in the government.

Photo by J. G. Fuller/The Hutchison Library

A banner carrying the red dragon—a traditional Welsh symbol—flies at Caerphilly Castle in southeastern Wales. Pre-Christian Celts may have first displayed the red dragon, which later became associated with the legends of King Arthur. The British monarch allows the emblem to be flown throughout Wales, even though there is an official flag for the United Kingdom.

The national legislature has two parts. The democratically elected House of Commons is more powerful than the hereditary House of Lords. The Commons has members from England, Wales, Scotland, and Northern Ireland. In 1990 the House of Commons had 38 MPs from Wales, out of a total of 650 delegates. MPs retain their seats for the life of the Parliament to which they are elected. By law, Parliaments may not sit for more than five years at a time. General elections may be held at shorter intervals.

The members of the House of Lords, who neither receive a salary nor seek election, hold office because of their aristocratic, honorary, or religious titles. The Lords cannot prevent a bill passed by the Commons from becoming law, but the members can delay certain legislation for up to one year. The House of Lords can also offer amendments to proposed laws, returning their ideas to the Commons for a final vote.

The Welsh judicial system is based on parliamentary legislation and common law. Serious offenses are tried before the Crown Court, which consists of a judge and a jury. Magistrate courts, which justices of the peace operate, and county courts hear less serious cases. A decision by a magistrate court can be appealed to the Crown Court or the High Court. At the top of the judicial system are nine judges from the House of Lords, who deal with appeals from lower courts.

For administrative purposes, Wales is divided into eight counties, which are further split into districts. The secretary of state for Wales, who is a member of the national cabinet, heads the Welsh Office. It has responsibility for affairs in the principality. Centered in Cardiff, the Welsh Office oversees health services, education up to the university level, environmental protection, and city and country planning. Policies relating to agriculture, forestry, fishing, and urban renewal also come under the authority of the Welsh Office.

A shepherd watches his flock in the hills of Dyfed, a county in western Wales. Raising sheep or other livestock is a common livelihood for many rural Welsh people.

3) The People

More than 2.8 million people live in Wales, out of a total of 57 million inhabitants in the United Kingdom. Although Wales's overall density is 350 people per square mile, the population is not evenly distributed. Some urban areas of southeastern Wales are very crowded, while rural parts of the north and west are sparsely settled.

Ethnic Identity

Most Welsh people, even those who do not speak Welsh, take great pride in their Celtic ancestry. Celtic festivals are well attended, and parents still name their children after Celtic heroes and heroines. Signposts throughout Wales appear in Welsh as well as in English. The very name of the people, however, suggests how difficult the struggle to maintain a Welsh identity has been. The word *Welsh* is not of Celtic origin but comes from an Anglo-Saxon term for foreigner. Historically, Welsh Celts called themselves *Cymry*, which means "friend."

Areas within the rugged Welsh uplands have maintained ties with their Celtic origins more easily than have lowland regions that have been overrun by outsiders. In recent years, however, tourism has reached even into northern Wales, where many English people now spend their vacations. The presence of more English-speakers has caused the use of the Welsh

An older Welshman walks his dog on the streets of Caernarvon. Roughly 20 percent of Wales's population is over the age of 65. This percentage is rising as more retired people from other parts of the United Kingdom buy homes in Wales.

language—a major feature of Welsh identity—to decrease.

In some senses, the Welsh lifestyle differs little from that of other British citizens. A majority of Welsh people can afford to own their homes, and two out of three have cars. Most jobs in Wales are in the manufacturing and service sectors, which dominate the cities and towns of the south. In rural areas, farming and herding are common occupations. As in England and Scotland, the custom of drinking tea in the late afternoon occurs in urban businesses as well as in country kitchens. In the evenings, people from all walks of life visit public houses (pubs), where locally brewed beer is served along with traditional foods and snacks.

Language and Religion

Since 1967, Wales has had two official languages—Welsh and English. In that year, Welsh gained equality with English in all legal senses. Until that time, Welsh could not be used in court or for government business. Most people—especially those at the upper levels of Welsh society—speak English. About 20 percent of the entire population use both Welsh and English. A very small percentage speak only Welsh. The Welsh-speakers tend to live in western and northwestern areas, which historically have been least influenced by English culture.

Of Celtic origin, Welsh shares roots with tongues spoken in Scotland, Ireland, and Brittany (a section of northeastern France that also was settled by Celts). Although invaders influenced the language, it remains tied to its ancient beginnings. The earliest form of Welsh dates from about A.D. 550. It remained in use until the late 700s, when Old Welsh developed. In the twelfth century, a new form of the language—called Middle Welsh—came into use. From it developed Modern Welsh, which emerged in the late 1400s.

In the eighth century, the Welsh adopted the Latin alphabet (in which English is also written) to set down their own language. Nevertheless, the letters *k, q, v,* and *z* do not appear in Welsh, and it has specially pronounced characters, such as the double *l* and the double *d.* In addition, *w* is occasionally used as a vowel. Welsh place names, some of which are very descriptive, are difficult for English-speakers to say. An unusual example is Llanfairpwllgwyngyll-gogerychwyrndrobwllllantysiliogogogoch, a village on Anglesey. The name translates as "St. Mary's Church in a hollow of white hazel close to a rapid whirlpool and St. Tysilio's Church near a red cave."

In the sixteenth century, Welsh came to be used in church services, and composers began to write hymns in the language. Methodist and Baptist chapels sprang up throughout the country in the 1700s and 1800s and contributed to the growth of choirs that sang in Welsh. Later, newspapers and other publications appeared in the language. In the modern era, there has been renewed interest in preserving Welsh. In 1982 this revival resulted in the founding of Sianel 4 Cymru (Channel 4 Wales), a television station that broadcasts in Welsh at peak times.

Until 1914, the state religion of Wales was the Anglican Church, a Protestant

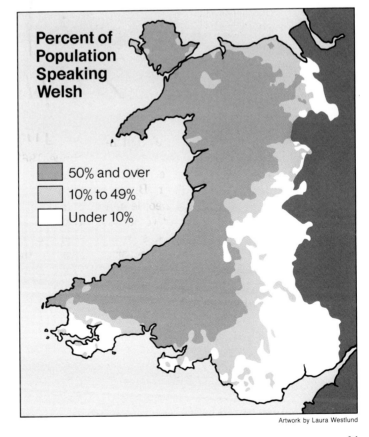

Percent of Population Speaking Welsh

- 50% and over
- 10% to 49%
- Under 10%

The decline in the number of Welsh-speakers began in the 1800s and continued through the 1900s. This chart shows the distribution of Welsh-speakers in Wales in the late 1980s. High percentages of people in northern and western Wales speak Welsh, but these areas are sparsely populated. By contrast, the east and south have the lowest percentages of Welsh-speakers but contain the largest populations. In the country as a whole, about 20 percent of the population speak Welsh.

Artwork by Laura Westlund

sect that is the official religious organization in England. At that time, however, more than 80 percent of the Welsh population followed non-Anglican religions. The Welsh Church Act of 1914 disestablished (separated) the church in Wales, making the country's Anglican Church a private, not a state, institution.

The majority of Welsh people follow Protestant sects that are called nonconformist or free churches because they do not have ties to the state. The Methodists maintain the largest congregation in Wales. Other nonconformist sects in the country include the Presbyterian, Baptist, and United Reform churches. A small number of Anglicans continue to practice their faith in Wales, and about 5 percent of the people are Roman Catholics.

Music and Art

In the nineteenth century, a cultural movement revived the *eisteddfod* (Welsh for "a session"), an ancient contest for Welsh

Courtesy of British Tourist Authority

Wearing a traditional folk costume, a young girl participates in the International Music Eisteddfod—a celebration of Welsh music and dance. Held each July at Llangollen, the eisteddfod includes daytime competitions and evening concerts.

Courtesy of Britain on View

In the presence of spectators and officials, young dancers perform at the National Eisteddfod. Although similar to the international festival, the national celebration is conducted entirely in Welsh.

A harpist plucks a melody outside the walls of Harlech Castle in western Wales.

bards (singer-poets). There are two annual eisteddfods in Wales. Conducted in Welsh, the National Eisteddfod is held in a different place in Wales each year, alternating between a northern and a southern locality. This festival brings together many elements of Welsh arts—poetry, music, and song—in a competition to choose the best bards, musicians, and singers for the year. The International Music Eisteddfod, always held in the village of Llangollen, is a more general celebration of Welsh culture and arts.

A favorite instrument of the bards was the harp, which has a long history in Wales. Eventually, harps became part of a larger group of instruments, including fiddles and organs, played to accompany folk songs and religious hymns. In 1945 the Welsh National Opera Company was founded, and it has become internationally acclaimed for its performances of new and traditional operas in many languages.

As the number of Welsh-speakers declined in the 1900s, the people's interest

The Welsh artist Peter Prendergast painted the landscape near Bethesda, a slate-quarrying town in northern Wales.

shifted from Welsh folk songs to popular music from England and the United States. English-speaking singers emerging in the 1950s and 1960s included Shirley Bassey and Tom Jones. She comes from Cardiff, and he was born in Pontypridd. Dafydd Iwan reached Welsh-speaking audiences in the same period. The performances and recordings by all-male Welsh choirs have remained popular in the late twentieth century.

Some well-known Welsh painters, such as Richard Wilson in the 1700s, worked in England or Europe for most of their lives. In the twentieth century, the public came to know the work of several Welsh artists. Trained in London, Augustus John used vivid colors to bring out his bold designs. The art of Ceri Richards shows the influence of European painters, although his inspirations included London street people and Welsh poetry.

Literature

Wales has a long history of literature in Welsh, but for centuries advancement in a religious, political, or legal career required fluent skill in Latin or English. As a result, most people at the upper levels of Welsh society wrote and spoke only those languages. These Welsh produced poetry, novels, plays, essays, histories, and travel books.

WELSH WRITERS IN WELSH

The earliest literature in Welsh was poetry that was memorized rather than written down. In about A.D. 600, the poet Aneirin composed *Y Gododdin*, an exciting story of brave warriors fighting the Anglo-Saxons. Several Welsh authors of the twelfth century wrote epic tales, or sagas, which describe the activities of Welsh heroes and heroines. Some of these stories were later collected in *The Mabinogion*. Using complex poetic forms, Dafydd ap Gwilym outshone other Welsh writers of the 1300s.

Courtesy of Welsh Arts Council

Two actors perform in the Welsh National Opera's production of *The Barber of Seville* by Gioacchino Antonio Rossini. Composed in 1816, this comic opera has many funny characters.

Independent Picture Service

Born in Cardiff in 1937, Shirley Bassey began her career by singing in small nightclubs. By the 1970s, her dynamic style had won fans throughout Britain and the United States. Bassey has made a number of successful albums but is mostly known for her lively concerts.

After the establishment of the Anglican Church in the 1500s, two important books appeared in Welsh. The Book of Common Prayer, which was the main Anglican prayerbook, came out in 1567. Bishop William Morgan used traditional poetic rhythms in his translation of the Bible in 1588. His work contributed greatly to the survival of the Welsh language. In the eighteenth century, another religious writer—the Methodist leader William Williams of Pantycelyn—composed hymns and religious essays in Welsh.

In the 1800s, Welsh writers included the poet Islwyn (born William Thomas) and Daniel Owen, who wrote novels that examined the effects of the industrial age on Welsh life. Nationalism became a feature of Welsh literature in the twentieth century. Saunders Lewis, an early president of Plaid Cymru, criticized the decline of Welsh culture in a variety of essays. In 1962 he inspired young Welsh-speakers to save Welsh from extinction in his famous radio broadcast, "The Fate of the Language." For more than 50 years, Kate Roberts wrote movingly about life in northwestern Wales in her finely crafted short stories.

Independent Picture Service

William Williams of Pantycelyn helped the Welsh language to survive in the 1700s by writing many beautiful hymns and by preaching in Welsh.

WELSH WRITERS IN OTHER LANGUAGES

In the twelfth century, two of the most famous writers from Wales were Geoffrey of Monmouth and Giraldus Cambrensis (Gerald the Welshman). Both composed in Latin, the language of scholars and of the Roman Catholic Church. In about 1136, Geoffrey finished *Historia regum Britanniae (History of the Kings of Britain),* which identified King Arthur as a Welsh ruler. Giraldus, who branded Geoffrey's work as fiction, described Wales in two famous travel books.

Although English-speaking, Welsh-born authors (called Anglo-Welsh) have produced many works in English since the sixteenth century, the 1900s have been the busiest period. This outpouring is partly because of the influence of English culture on Wales in the 1800s, when the number of Welsh-speakers began to decline.

The most famous Anglo-Welsh writer is Dylan Thomas. Born in Swansea in 1914,

Independent Picture Service

Among modern, English-speaking writers, the Welshman Dylan Thomas *(pictured with his wife, Caitlin)* is recognized for his passionate poetry and for his unusual use of words and sounds.

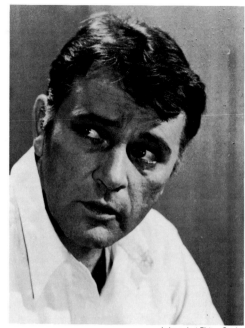

The Welsh actors Emlyn Williams *(left)* and Richard Burton *(right)* had very similar backgrounds. Both were born in poor circumstances, and both were helped to success by dedicated teachers. Williams also wrote plays and gave Burton one of his first acting jobs. Burton later became an acclaimed classical performer but also appeared in works that had a popular appeal.

Thomas could not speak Welsh. Nevertheless, like Welsh-speaking poets, he was intrigued by the sound of words and used passionate, stirring language to convey humor, sadness, and love. His first publication to gain widespread recognition was *18 Poems,* followed by *Portrait of the Artist as a Young Dog.* Among his most famous works is his play *Under Milk Wood,* which a fellow Welshman—the actor Richard Burton—performed on the radio soon after Thomas's death in 1953. The play describes a typical day in the lives of the unusual inhabitants of a small Welsh port.

Some twentieth-century writers idealized the Wales of previous times. Richard Llewellyn gave a sentimental account of life in a mining community in *How Green Was My Valley.* In a similar vein, the playwright and actor Emlyn Williams told the story of his Welsh boyhood in *The Corn Is Green.* Both of these works became feature films. The publications of more recent writers, such as R. S. Thomas and Emyr Humphreys, reflect pride in their unique Welsh culture and concern for its survival.

Health and Welfare

Since 1945, Wales has been part of a welfare state—that is, a nation where the government provides for the well-being of all its citizens. A major part of this effort is the National Health Service, which offers most medical services at minimal cost to patients. This comprehensive program has brought many diseases under control.

The National Health Service has also helped to lower the number of Welsh children who die within the first year of life. At 9 deaths per 1,000 live births, the infant mortality rate is now among the lowest in the world. The average life expectancy for a Welsh person is 74.

The major health threats in Wales are stroke, cancer, and heart disease. To combat heart disease, the Welsh office of the National Health Service began "Heartbeat Wales." This pioneering program has influenced other community efforts in Britain to prevent the illness.

Another aspect of the welfare state is the system that provides funds to the elderly, the sick, the disabled, and the unemployed. Government spending in this area has risen dramatically in recent years be-

cause of high unemployment. Some Welsh people, particularly youth from the southern cities, live off their welfare checks for long periods—a situation called "being on the dole."

Education

Wales has its own educational system, and all Welsh children between the ages of 5

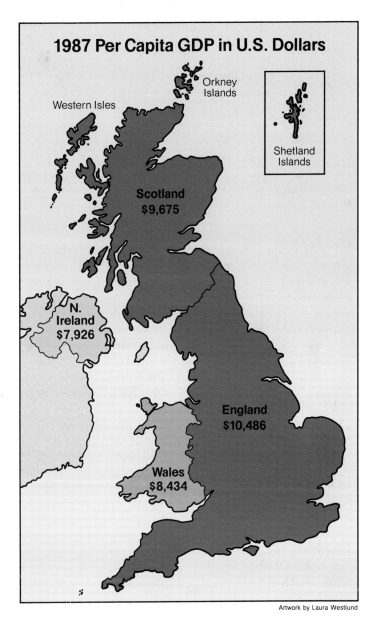

1987 Per Capita GDP in U.S. Dollars

Western Isles

Orkney Islands

Shetland Islands

Scotland
$9,675

N. Ireland
$7,926

England
$10,486

Wales
$8,434

This map compares the average productivity per person—calculated by gross domestic product (GDP) per capita—for the four countries that make up the United Kingdom. The GDP is the value of all goods and services produced within the borders of each country in a year. To arrive at the GDP per capita, each country's total GDP is divided by its population. The resulting dollar amounts indicate one measure of the quality of life in Britain. The overall GDP figure for the United Kingdom is $10,239. The figure for Wales is lower, reflecting the country's difficulty in adjusting to new economic circumstances. Nevertheless, free medical care and other welfare services give most Welsh people a good standard of living. (Data taken from *Britain 1990,* prepared by the Central Office of Information.)

Artwork by Laura Westlund

and 16 must attend school. Since Wales is a bilingual country (meaning it has two official languages), students can take courses in either English or Welsh. More than 95 percent of the population can read and write in at least one language.

Most children go to schools that the government funds. A small number of Welsh pupils attend private schools, which charge fees. Primary school lasts until roughly age 11, and secondary-school students complete their studies at 16. Most secondary schools are comprehensives—that is, they provide a wide range of courses and do not distinguish between pupils according to ability. Some schools use Welsh as the main language of teaching, while in other institutions Welsh is a secondary subject.

After they finish compulsory schooling, Welsh students have a variety of educa-tional options. If they qualify, graduates can attend any of Britain's vocational and technical colleges or academic universi-ties. Among the most unusual schools in the United Kingdom is the Open Univer-sity, which was founded in 1969. This in-stitution has no regular campus and offers its courses on television, on radio, on video cassettes, and through the mail.

Within their own country, Welsh stu-dents can enroll at the University of Wales. This institution runs seven campuses—one each at Aberystwyth, Bangor, Swansea, and Lampeter, and three in Cardiff. The total enrollment of the University of Wales is 20,000.

Sports

In 1880, when the Welsh Rugby Union was established, the sport of rugby gained

Students relax in a courtyard of the Bangor campus of the University of Wales. Dating mostly from the late 1800s and early 1900s, the university's buildings occupy the newest part of town.

A lone climber scales one of the rugged hills near Capel Curig in Snowdonia National Park.

official recognition. It has since become an important part of Welsh culture. Originating in England, rugby is a fast-moving game. Players wear no padding and engage in exciting runs, athletic catches, and long kicks to reach their opponents' goal line. There are 13 members per side in amateur rugby matches, and professional teams have 15 people on each side. In Wales, the sport is fiercely competitive, especially when the Welsh team plays against the English team. At these meetings, Welsh fans wear leeks on their lapels and sing "Hen Wlad fy Nhadau" ("Land of My Fathers"), the Welsh national anthem.

Other athletic activities, such as soccer (called football in Wales), have also become very popular. Through the Football Association of Wales, the country supports both professional and amateur soccer teams. Cricket, another sport from England, is also played throughout Wales. This bat-and-ball game pits two 11-member teams against one another. Walking, climbing, gardening, and fishing are among the leisure activities that attract outdoor enthusiasts.

Food

Living in an environment in which farming is not easy, the Welsh have developed foods based on livestock and products from the sea. Because so many livestock

Welsh athletes struggle against a French team in a game of rugby. The sport is physically rough and a source of great national interest in Wales.

graze on Welsh grasslands, meat, such as bacon and lamb, appears often in the Welsh diet. *Cawl,* a one-pot meal, means "broth" in Welsh and consists of bacon and vegetables in a thin soup.

Fish have long been an important source of protein, and fried herring and mackerel are popular. The ingredients for two Welsh seafood delicacies—cockles and laver—are increasingly hard to find. A small shellfish, cockles were long collected off the coast of southern Wales. Also available in this region is laver, an edible seaweed. Welsh cooks prepare laver into a breakfast food called *bara lawr,* or laverbread, by sprin-

kling it with oatmeal and frying it in bacon fat. In recent years, however, the hauls of cockles and laver have decreased as birds and overfishing have depleted stocks.

Another favorite dish, which has become popular in other parts of the United Kingdom as well, is Welsh rarebit (also called Welsh rabbit). Often referred to as toasted cheese, this easy meal consists of melted cheese and spices on top of a piece of toast. The most famous cheese to come from Wales is Caerphilly, named after a town in Mid Glamorgan. This crumbly, white cheese is now made both in Wales and England.

Although originally a Welsh dish, *caws pobi*—also called Welsh rarebit—has become popular throughout Britain.

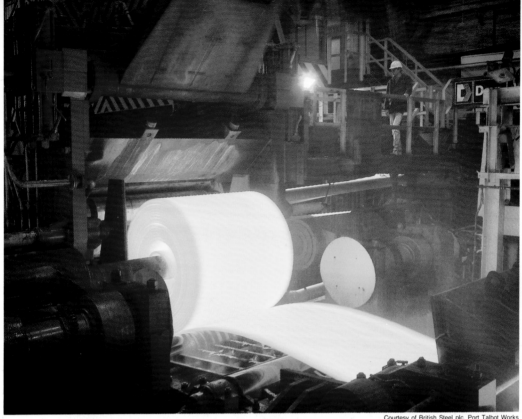

Updated in the mid-1980s, the steelworks at Port Talbot make heavy goods. Here, a worker wearing a hard hat monitors the red-hot steel as machines wrap it into a thick coil.

4) The Economy

As part of the United Kingdom, Wales participates in an economy that is dependent on trade and manufacturing. For more than a century, Wales provided coal (as fuel) and slate and iron ore (as building materials) to support industrial endeavors. By the mid-1930s, however, the Welsh economy was faltering. Coal, iron ore, and slate lost their economic importance, and many workers lost their jobs when mines, quarries, and factories closed. In the 1980s, the unemployment rate had risen to as much as 50 percent in some parts of southern Wales. Secondary-school graduates had little hope of finding work, and many ended up on the welfare list.

The national government's solution to Wales's economic problems was to name some areas as special development districts. These regions received funds to broaden their industries, to establish new factories, and to retrain workers. This widespread effort has attracted many businesses to Wales. About 20 percent of all foreign companies setting up branches in the United Kingdom go to Wales.

More than 90 percent of the Welsh work force is employed in manufacturing and in the service sector, which includes areas such as construction, banking, tourism, communications, and the retail trade. Only small percentages of Welsh people remain involved in farming and mining—the two activities that once employed most of the country's citizens.

Manufacturing and Mining

After 1945, when World War II was over, public attention in Wales turned to jobs and to the industries that had been depressed before the war began in 1939. Southern Wales—for decades the source of the country's jobs and wealth—declined as mines and factories closed. The British government took over the coal and steel industries, which adapted to the changing circumstances by expanding into other areas of manufacturing.

In addition to steelworks and tin-plating plants, Wales began to attract firms that produced electronic equipment, consumer goods, and chemicals. The government helped to build industrial parks, or estates, and in time these vast manufacturing concentrations drew foreign businesses, primarily from Japan and the United States. They set up factories in Shotton, Barry, and the Rhondda Valley that produced car parts, computer equipment, plastics, stainless steel, paper goods, and synthetic fabrics.

An unusual manufacturing area emerged in the 1970s, when the natural harbor at Milford Haven became a hub of oil refining. International and national companies own the refining facilities, which are located within Pembrokeshire Coast National Park. Milford Haven is now one of Britain's main oil ports and refines the oil

Courtesy of British Steel plc. Port Talbot Works

At a finishing mill *(left),* machines reduce a 1.3-inch bar of steel to an extremely thin rod that leaves the production line at 35 miles per hour. Many factories have been built in vast industrial estates, such as the one at Treforest *(below),* near the capital.

Independent Picture Service

The bright lights of Milford Haven's dock facilities reflect off oil tankers unloading their cargo.

The Japanese managing director of a Panasonic plant stands in front of the factory, which is located near Newport in southern Wales. Workers at the plant produce typewriters, printers, and telephones.

The narrow and dangerous working conditions *(left)* of miners have improved considerably since the early 1900s. In modern times, laborers have access to sophisticated machinery *(below)*.

taken from the North Sea, which lies east and north of England and Scotland. The port's deepwater terminal can handle tankers that carry more than 200,000 tons of cargo. Additional refining facilities exist near Swansea.

For most of the twentieth century, Wales's mining industries have experienced hard times. Part of the decline is due to the increased use of oil and hydropower —instead of coal—for industrial and domestic energy. In addition, the coal deposits of southern Wales are nearly exhausted. Only about a dozen coal mines still operate in the region, and a few mines in northern Wales supply local factories. Workers continue to extract small amounts of limestone, slate, and gold in Wales, but most manufacturers now import their raw materials, including iron and steel.

Agriculture, Forestry, and Fishing

Lacking large expanses of low, fertile land, Wales accommodates many small farms that usually cover less than 150 acres. Most of these holdings are used to raise sheep and dairy and beef cattle, although a few farms in southwestern Wales and on Anglesey grow crops.

In the lowlands of the coast and inland valleys, farmers plant hay and other crops to feed their livestock. Friesians are a common type of dairy cattle, and many beef cattle belong to the Welsh Black breed. Sheep—often the Welsh Mountain variety—stay in the elevated moorlands of central Wales, where the grass provides plentiful pasture. The animals once were raised for the wool industry but have increasingly become a major source of meat.

Because crop farming is very limited, Wales is not self-sufficient in food. The country must import many products from other parts of Britain and from abroad to supplement Welsh harvests of barley, oats, and potatoes. The leek has long been used to flavor Welsh soups and stews. Additional vegetables grown in Wales include rutabagas and other turnips.

Only about 11 percent of Wales is forested. The main concentrations of trees are located in areas where poor soil has discouraged farming and pasturing. The Forestry Commission has encouraged the planting of many trees, favoring pine, spruce, and larch, which mature faster than the slow-growing hardwoods. The commission's efforts are focused on providing more softwood trees for commercial purposes. Most of the timber is used in the building and pulp industries.

Fishing was once an important occupation for the Welsh because of the country's

Photo by Sian Roderick

Workers at a livestock market in Brecon move sheep from their pens in preparation for sale.

Stacks of grain lean on each other during harvesttime in the Conwy Valley of northern Wales.

easy access to the sea. The wealth of sea inlets gave rise to many fishing ports, notably Fishguard, Tenby, and Conwy. Seafood remains prominent in the Welsh diet, but the number of people working in the fishing industry dropped in the 1980s. The total British catch exceeds 700,000 tons annually.

Most commercial fishermen in Wales catch whitefish (cod, plaice, and skate) and shellfish. Because the supply of whitefish has dropped, shellfish now form a more important haul. Although the cockle population has declined, the town of Penclawdd is still the leading Welsh center for the cockle industry.

Trees dominate the landscape of this section of central Wales. About 12 percent of the country is forested, and an active tree-planting program is under way.

Buyers bid for catches of mackerel and shellfish in Milford Haven.

A fisherman paddles his small boat, called a coracle, on the Teifi River. Of ancient design, coracles are still used because they can turn quickly in the water.

57

Tourism

In the 1800s, wealthy people traveled to Wales, establishing Llandudno, Tenby, and Aberystwyth as popular resorts. As the British have acquired more income and more leisure time, tourism has become a big business in Wales. The country earns more than $800 million from tourism each year, and the industry provides roughly 80,000 jobs.

Of the 12 million people who vacation in Wales annually, large numbers travel to the northern countryside. This trend has sparked tension, because some local residents resent the English people who own holiday cottages in the region. Many Welsh feel that tourism, while an important source of money, endangers their fragile culture.

Major attractions in Wales include the Norman castles that date from the time of Edward I. National festivals, mainly the eisteddfods, draw people who are interested in experiencing the Celtic traditions of Wales. Outdoor enthusiasts enjoy the country's rugged beauty. Some climb the slopes of Snowdon, and others go on long-distance walks.

Hikers enjoy the rugged terrain of Snowdonia National Park, which covers 840 square miles in northwestern Wales. The park offers some of Britain's best trails for walking, hiking, and climbing.

Anglers practice fly fishing on a river in western Wales.

Visitors also come to Wales for its scenic beauty, including Three Cliffs, a sandy beach on the Gower Peninsula.

Chepstow Castle *(left)* lies just inside the Welsh border in southeastern Wales. The remains of Caerphilly Castle *(below)* also draw many tourists. Both castles date from the Norman period (eleventh to thirteenth centuries), when French-speaking nobles took over large areas of southern Wales.

Courtesy of Richard Rodgers

Courtesy of British Tourist Authority

Courtesy of Richard Rodgers

A spinner displays his ancient craft at the Welsh Folk Museum outside Cardiff. The museum's many open-air exhibits preserve parts of Welsh culture, showing visitors how items such as cloth, flour, and wool were made before the industrial age.

Transportation and Energy

Like the rest of the United Kingdom, Wales has a well-developed transportation network. Much of it was put together in the 1800s, when new forms of travel—such as railways—revolutionized overland movement. Well-paved roads, smooth-running railways, and water transport connect most parts of the country.

Wales has more than 30,000 miles of roads. The highways and trunk roads link cities in southern, northern, and eastern Wales. Good connections also exist between Wales and the main urban hubs of England. In central and western Wales, narrow, two-lane routes form a secondary overland network.

In the 1800s, railways first made their appearance in Wales and were used to transport people and freight. In the modern era, these lines have been upgraded and now carry millions of passengers every year. Comfortable, 125-mile-per-hour diesel trains bring people from Cardiff and Newport to London in about two hours. Another major line goes through northern Wales to Holyhead near Anglesey to connect with passenger boats to Ireland. Slower trains run between smaller locations throughout the country.

Photo by E. Emrys Jones/Y Drych

Ferries link the Welsh port of Holyhead near Anglesey to Dublin, Ireland. Here, passengers drive their cars off the *St. Columba,* a vessel named after a sixth-century Irish monk.

Independent Picture Service

Most secondary roads in Wales are narrow and connect small towns.

Although Wales contains many natural harbors, most of them are small. The largest ports are at Milford Haven, Swansea, Cardiff, Port Talbot, and Newport. Mainly an oil port, Milford Haven also handles products made from petroleum at its vast dock facilities. Over 30 million tons of goods leave Milford Haven every year. The other ports in southern Wales generally ship manufactured goods to Europe and North America.

Western England depends on Wales for much of its energy. Coal-powered and oil-fired facilities exist, as do hydropower stations and nuclear reactors. Hydroelectric dams produce power along the country's rivers, notably on the Severn. Located within the Elan Valley, the Severn's facilities provide electricity to the English metropolitan area of Birmingham. Nuclear reactors are located on Anglesey and near Snowdon. Natural gas plants near Wrexham provide energy to areas of northern Wales and western England.

Photo by Mark Richards/Brace Harvatt

A container vessel glides past oil-storage tanks at Milford Haven. A fine natural harbor, Milford Haven can accommodate ships both at low tide and at high tide. Foreign oil companies maintain their own dock facilities, refineries, and storage areas at the port. There are also independent companies that see to the needs of non-oil shippers.

Courtesy of Britain on View

Dams throughout the country supply power to Wales and to neighboring England. The Elan Valley contains several facilities that use the flow of the Severn River to produce electricity.

The sculptor Glenn Hellmann designed this modern memorial to Llywelyn II, the last native-born Prince of Wales. The work commemorates the 700th anniversary of Llywelyn's death in 1282. The bird on top of the memorial is a reminder of the prince's nickname—"Eagle of Eagles from the Land of the Eagles." Despite centuries of British rule, the Welsh have a strong sense of their country's separate place in Britain's history.

Courtesy of Welsh Arts Council

The Future

Economic concerns overshadow the future of Wales. Once humming with activity, the country has had to face the problems of rising unemployment and mine closures in recent years. Financial incentives have attracted many foreign investors to the country, and these new firms are helping to lift Wales from its economic slump.

Yet, with the arrival of newcomers, some Welsh people wonder whether their culture can survive if it opens its doors to outsiders. This concern has provoked objections to the presence of English vacationers and foreign businesses. As a result, balancing Welsh economic and cultural desires will remain one of the greatest challenges for Wales in the 1990s.

Index